Public Schools
Library Protection Act 1998

SCIENCE PROJECT IDEAS

Science Project Ideas About

ANIMAL
BEHAVIOR

Robert Gardner and David Webster

Enslow Publishers, Inc.
40 Industrial Road   PO Box 38
Box 398   Aldershot
Berkeley Heights, NJ 07922   Hants GU12 6BP
USA   UK
http://www.enslow.com

Library of Congress Cataloging-in-Publication Data

Gardner, Robert, 1929–
    Science project ideas about animal behavior / Robert Gardner and
David Webster.
        p. cm.—(Science project ideas)
    Summary: Presents facts about animal behavior and includes related
experiments, projects, and activities.
    ISBN 0-89490-842-1
    1. Animal behavior—Experiments—Juvenile literature. 2. Zoology
projects—Juvenile literature. [1. Animals—Habits and behavior—
Experiments. 2. Experiments. 3. Science projects.] I. Webster, David,
1930– . II. Title. III. Series: Gardner, Robert, 1929–   Science project
ideas.
QL751.5.G375 1997
591.5—dc2l   97-13136
                                                    CIP
                                                    AC

Printed in the United States of America

10 9 8 7 6 5 4

Illustration Credits: Jacob Katari

Photo Credits: © Corel Corporation, p. 23.

Cover Photo: Jerry McCrea

CONTENTS

INTRODUCTION

In this book you will find experiments about the behavior of animals, including humans, the animal with whom you are most familiar. The experiments use simple everyday materials and animals that are readily available.

The book will help you to understand how real scientists work. You will be answering questions by doing experiments that demonstrate basic scientific principles. You will also read about how several scientists designed and carried out experiments to try to explain the behavior of several animals, particularly owls and honeybees.

Most of the experiments you do will provide detailed guidance. But some of them will raise questions and ask you to make up your own experiments to answer them. An experiment of this kind could be the start of a good science fair project. Such experiments are marked with an asterisk (*).

Please note: **If an experiment uses anything that has a potential for danger, you will be asked to work with an adult.** Please do so! The purpose of this teamwork is to prevent you from being hurt.

Science Project Ideas About Animal Behavior can open science's door for you—and make you glad that you are a human among all the other animals!

MEASUREMENT ABBREVIATIONS

centimeter	cm	inch	in
foot	ft	meter	m

Man is a reasoning animal.
(Seneca)

1
WAYS OF KNOWING

Many people believe that humans represent the most advanced stage of animal evolution. It is true that we can learn to talk, read, write, and reason. Most importantly, we can pass on what we learn to future generations through books, films, letters, photographs, and many other means. Yet, other animals have skills that are superior to ours. A gazelle, a horse, a bear, and many other animals can run faster than we can. Most mammals have a much better sense of smell than we do. The eagle's keen eyesight is far better than ours. We can hear only those sounds between 20 and 20,000 vibrations per second, while dogs can hear sounds from 15 to 50,000 vibrations per second. Bats, who use the echoes of sounds to locate their prey, can hear sounds of 1,000 to 120,000 vibrations per second, and dolphins can hear sounds of 150 to 150,000 vibrations per second. Figure 1 is a graph that shows the range of hearing and voice sounds for several different animals.

A dog's ability to hear very high pitched sounds—sounds with more than 20,000 vibrations per second—is the basis for dog whistles. When a dog owner blows such a whistle, we cannot hear it. But a dog can hear these sounds and will respond if properly trained.

Many animals see light that we cannot see. Rattlesnakes can see infrared light, which we can only sense as heat. They use this added range of sight to find their prey at night. Many insects can see ultraviolet light that we cannot detect without the aid of instruments. Their ability to see this light helps them find nectar and pollen on flowers that reflect ultraviolet light.

Nocturnal animals—animals that are active at night—have an extra layer of tissue

Figure 1

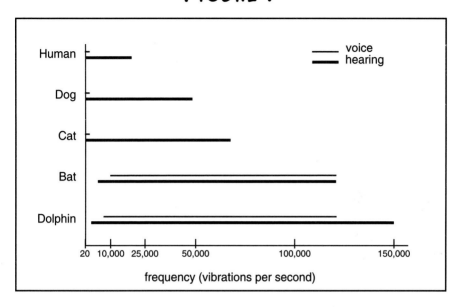

This graph shows the frequency of sounds (the number of vibrations per second) that can be heard and made (voice) by five different animals. As you can see, humans can hear and make only a very small range of sounds.

at the very back of their eyes. This layer reflects light back through the retina, the membrane that receives the image. Some of the light that was not absorbed as it passed through the retina the first time is absorbed on the second trip. The added light due to reflection enables cats to see better. It is this reflected light that makes the eyes of a cat or raccoon glow at night when light strikes their eyes.

While a dog's sense of smell is probably a thousand times better than ours, a fish is a thousand times more sensitive to odors than a dog. This means that a fish's sense of smell is a million times better than ours.

Salmon always return to spawn in the same stream in which they hatched. Some scientists believed that the fish use their keen sense of smell to find their way home. To test this idea, a number of salmon were captured in a stream. They were then taken downstream below the fork in the river where they had originally gone to the left. Next, half the salmon had their noses stuffed with cotton. Both the salmon who could smell and those who could not smell were marked so they could be identified. The salmon were then released. After swimming upstream, they again reached the same fork in the river. The salmon who could smell all chose the left fork again. Of the salmon who could not smell, half chose the left fork and half chose the right fork. This would be expected by chance. Without their sense of smell, they could not identify their "home."

Some organisms—such as birds, whales, and even some bacteria—have built-in magnets that help them find their way along the earth's surface. Homing pigeons released near an iron mine where there is a strong magnetic field may have difficulty beginning their homeward flight. They may fly some distance from the mine before turning and flying toward home. If a tiny but strong magnet is attached to a pigeon's body, the magnet interferes with the bird's ability to detect the earth's magnetic field. Nevertheless, on a sunny day pigeons with attached magnets will quickly head for home. But on cloudy days they fly in random directions. This suggests that they can use the sun, as well as the earth's magnetic field, to navigate.

Some bacteria have magnetic crystals containing iron in their tiny single-celled bodies. Normally, these bacteria move in a northerly direction. Placing a strong magnet near the bacteria can cause them to reverse their direction of travel. If iron is removed from their environment, their cells are soon without iron. Lacking iron, they no longer move in a northerly direction. Instead, their movements become random.

You may have heard someone say that only humans can communicate. But you know that is not true. If communication is the giving of information by one animal to another so as to benefit one or both of them, then a dog or a cat can communicate. A dog can certainly let you know when it wants to go outside. From experience, you know that a dog's wagging tail or a cat's purring shows contentment, while a growl or a hiss indicates dislike or signals a warning. The barking of a watchdog tells its owner that someone or something is approaching, and even a lowly cricket's chirping rate can be used to tell temperature.

Two Ways of Knowing

An animal's ability to respond to stimuli—things that cause a response (action)—may indicate either active or passive knowledge. Active knowledge is knowledge that is learned. Passive knowledge is not learned; it is innate. It consists of responses an animal is born with. Innate responses are built into an animal's nervous system by the genes it receives from its parents.

It is not always easy to decide whether a behavior is caused by active or passive knowledge. If an egg is removed from a goose's nest, the goose will use its bill to roll the egg back into the nest. This would appear to be learned behavior. The goose is acting in a reasonable way to regain an egg that was removed from the nest. But actually the behavior is innate. It is an inborn response to a stimulus. The response can be triggered by any egg, not just its own. In fact, a goose will roll lightbulbs, baseballs, and even flashlight batteries into its nest. The response seems to be strongest if the object is round, large, green, and spotted.

Stimuli that trigger such innate responses as egg rolling are called releasers. They cause the animal to "release" the innate behavior stored in its nervous system. Herring gull chicks will peck at their parents' beaks to obtain food. The stimulus that acts as a releaser for this pecking behavior is the horizontal motion of a narrow, vertical, colored object such as a parent bird's beak. (An adult herring gull has a red spot on its beak.) If a narrow wooden dowel (stick) with red stripes is held vertically and moved back and forth, chicks will peck at it the same as they peck at their parent's beak.

If the releaser is a chemical, it is called a pheromone. Many insects use pheromones to attract a mate. Bees have several different pheromones. One is used to signal an attack on an invader; a second to indicate alarm; a third to attract bees to food; another to identify the queen bee; and so on.

In the case of a goose rolling an egg, the releaser is the sight of an egg or an egglike object outside the nest. Even if the egg is then taken away, the goose still behaves in the same way. It goes through the same motions, which shows that the response is an innate behavior.

Interestingly, geese will carry out egg-rolling behavior only while their eggs are being incubated. Once the eggs hatch, a goose will not retrieve an egg or egglike object placed outside the nest.

Conditioned Learning

About a hundred years ago, Ivan Pavlov, a Russian scientist and Nobel Prize winner, was using dogs to study digestion. He had connected tubes to a dog in order to measure the saliva the dog produced when food was placed in its mouth (Figure 2a). Shortly after starting his experiments, Pavlov discovered that the dog would begin to salivate (form saliva) as soon as it heard food being prepared.

He then tried ringing a bell before the dog was fed. The dog soon learned that the bell meant food was coming. It would salivate as soon as it heard the bell (Figure 2b). Pavlov called this learning process "conditioning." The bell, the sound of food being prepared, or whatever was used to make the dog salivate before it received food, Pavlov called the conditioned stimulus (CS). The formation of

FIGURE 2

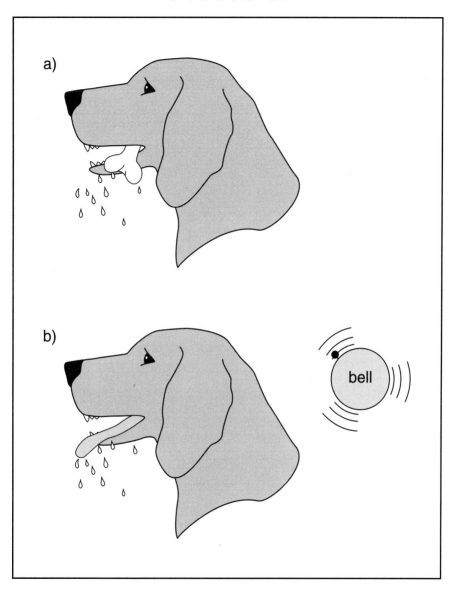

a) A dog salivates automatically when food is placed in its mouth.

b) After conditioning, a dog will salivate when it hears the conditioned stimulus (bell, can opener, or whatever it associates with being fed).

saliva by the dog in response to the bell (or any other CS), Pavlov called the conditioned response (CR).

Food alone was an unconditioned stimulus (US). Food placed in a dog's mouth caused the dog to secrete saliva. In this case, the formation of saliva is an unconditioned response (UR). Like you, a dog will salivate when food is placed in its mouth. Secretion of saliva is an automatic (unconditioned) response to food in the mouth. It is built-in (innate) behavior for both humans and dogs.

A lot of animal and human learning takes place through trial-and-error conditioning. We keep trying a number of things until something works. When it works, we repeat it because it provides the result we want. Learning to ride a bicycle or hit a ball are examples of trial-and-error learning. However, good coaching can help us to eliminate many of the errors we might otherwise make.

CONDITIONING YOUR DOG

To do this experiment you will need:

✔ stimulus such as bell, glass and spoon, whistle, etc.	✔ dog

If you have a dog, it may already be conditioned. For example, if you use a can opener to open dog food, the sound of the machine may be a conditioned stimulus. If your dog comes to the kitchen when it hears the can opener, it has probably learned that the sound means "dinnertime." It probably salivates (CR) when it hears the can opener (CS).

See if you can condition your dog to another stimulus. Try ringing a bell, whistling a particular tune, tapping a glass with a spoon, or using some other stimulus just before you feed your dog. If the dog is conditioned to another sound, such as the can opener, avoid using that stimulus. Open the can where the dog can't hear you.

Does the stimulus become a conditioned stimulus for the dog? How long does it take before the dog learns that the stimulus means food is coming?

Try to use conditioning to train your dog to shake hands, sit, stay, heel, roll over, and fetch the paper. Can you train your dog to do these things? to do other things?

*A bird came down the walk:
He did not know I saw.
(Emily Dickinson)*

2
SCIENCE AND ANIMAL BEHAVIOR

Trying to understand animal behavior is not easy. Animals can't tell us how they feel, what they think (if they think), or why they do what they do. They can't talk to us, or at least they don't speak a language that we can understand. Scientists who study animal behavior have to design clever experiments to try to find out why animals act the way they do.

17

This chapter will give you some idea of how a scientist attempts to understand animals. You will read about some of the clever experiments that have been done to try to understand animal behavior. Then you can try a couple of experiments on your own.

Many scientists study animals in the field. That is, they observe animals in their natural habitats (where the animals normally live). Other scientists conduct experiments in a laboratory. They bring animals to a laboratory and do experiments there.

In a laboratory, conditions can be controlled. The scientist doesn't have to worry about a predator devouring the animal being studied. Conditions such as temperature, humidity, length of day, intensity of light, and other factors can be kept constant or changed at will. On the other hand, removing an animal from its normal environment may change the way it behaves.

A Field Experiment

Many years ago, J. T. Emlen did a field experiment with cliff swallows. These birds use mud to build nests under cliffs and the eaves of buildings. Unlike most birds who defend a wide territory around their nests, cliff swallows build their nests next to one another in colonies, as shown in

FIGURE 3

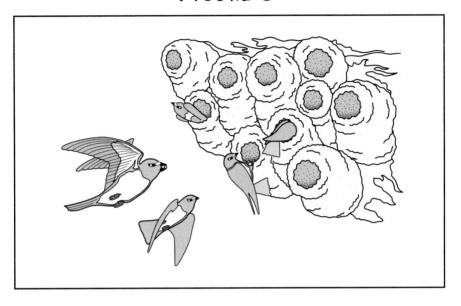

Cliff swallows build their nests in clusters, but each bird defends only its own nest.

Figure 3. Emlen wondered whether these birds would ever defend their nests.

Because the swallows looked so much alike, Emlen had to find a way to identify them in his experiment. He crept up close to the colony he was observing. From the top of the cliff, he used a toy water pistol to spray a few drops of quick-drying paint on specific birds. He could then use different colors or the different spray patterns to identify them.

Now that he could tell one swallow from another, he saw that the same birds always came to the same nests. They did not share their nests with other swallows. He wondered what would happen if two nests were joined. To find out, he waited until two birds he could identify were away from their adjoining nests. He then removed the wall between the nests. When the birds returned, they fought.

Based on the experiment, Emlen decided that cliff swallows do defend their territory. But unlike most birds, their territory is limited to the nest itself. Once the swallows rebuilt the wall, the fighting stopped.

A number of people have used binoculars to watch ground-nesting plovers. These birds will draw attention to themselves in order to protect their eggs or nesting young from predators. Their behavior would make us think that they are thinking as they draw predators away from their nests.

Sensing a threat, a plover will move slowly away from its eggs or young. If the threat continues, the plover will do one of several things. It may move through the grass, making squeaks that sound like a mouse. It may pretend to be sitting on a nest far from the real nest. When the invader draws near, the bird will fly away, leaving the false nest for the predator to examine. (Its flight will always be away from the real nest in case the predator chooses to chase the plover.) It may make loud calls to attract attention to itself if the predator is approaching the nest. Its most deceptive move is to pretend it has a broken wing and flop around noisily. The predator, sensing the plover is unable to fly, sprints to what it thinks is a quick meal. But just before it reaches the floundering plover, the bird takes flight, always in a direction away from its nest. Its return path to its chicks or eggs is never direct but roundabout.

The plover's behavior may be innate. But to an observer it certainly looks as though the bird is thinking of the best way to keep the predator from finding its nest (Figure 4).

FIGURE 4

This plover shows aggressive behavior toward a cow that is close to the bird's on-the-ground nest. The plover fears that the cow will step on the nest.

A Laboratory Experiment

Barn owls are valuable to farmers because they eat field mice that feed on orchard and garden crops (Figure 5). These birds are active at night. They usually remain quiet during the daytime. Roger Payne, who has studied many different animals, knew that barn owls feed almost exclusively on field mice. But how do they find their prey in darkness?

Even in daytime, field mice are hard to see because they build grass tunnels that cover their movements. It occurred to Payne that although mice do remain hidden most of the time, they must make noise as they move along their grass tunnels. Could it be that owls use their ears rather than their eyes to find field mice?

To find out, Payne set up an experiment. His laboratory was a large room in an old building. He carefully covered all the windows and cracks with boards, tape, and putty until he was sure that no light, not even bright sunlight, could enter the room. Since he planned to do his experiments at night in a lightproof room, he was certain that an owl could not use its eyes to find its prey. He spread leaves over the floor so that a mouse would make a rustling noise when it moved around the room.

FIGURE 5

A barn owl is shown with a mouse in its beak.

Payne obtained an owl that had always lived in captivity. After the owl had lived in the room a few days, Payne carried out his first experiment. He released a mouse into the dark room. Nothing happened! He turned on the lights, and the owl finally flew to the floor. But it didn't land on the mouse as owls usually do. Instead, it caught the mouse by running after it. Payne thought that because the owl had been raised in captivity, it had never seen its parents catch mice. It would have to learn how to hunt by itself. After a few trials with the lights on, the owl began to land directly on the mouse. Payne decided the owl had learned the proper way to hunt.

In his next experiment, Payne released a mouse into the dark room and waited. For an hour, the mouse barely moved. Then, at last, Payne heard it move slowly through the leaves. Seconds later he heard a thud. He turned on the lights. There was the owl with the mouse in its talons!

An hour later, he repeated the experiment with the same results. The owl, although raised in captivity, had learned to hunt very quickly after a few practice sessions in light. But was the owl really locating mice with its ears or did it smell the mouse? Perhaps the owl detected its prey by the heat radiating from the mouse's body. Could the owl, like rattlesnakes, have eyes that can see the infrared light released by warm bodies?

To find out if the owl detected the mouse by sensing heat or odor, Payne repeated the experiment using a cold "mouse." Actually, he used a wad of paper that he pulled along the floor with a string. If the owl was guided by heat or odor, it should not be able to find this cold mouse. Payne had barely started to pull the cold mouse along the floor when— *wham!*—the owl landed on the wad of paper. Payne had shown that the owl did not have to rely on infrared radiation or smell to locate its prey in darkness.

Of course, Payne had not proved that owls do not *use* smell to hunt their prey. He had simply shown that they do not *need* to use smell to find a mouse.

Perhaps the owl, like a bat, was locating its prey by sending out high-pitched sounds and then following the echoes. The echoes from a mouse would have to have a particular characteristic that the owl could recognize. Otherwise, it wouldn't know whether it was flying at a mouse, a lion, or a stone.

To see if the owl was using a sonar system similar to a bat's, Payne used a small loudspeaker to broadcast a recording of a mouse running through leaves. If the owl was using echoes, it would recognize that the sound reflected from the loudspeaker was different than the sound reflected from a mouse. The owl quickly (but disappointedly) landed on the loudspeaker. Obviously, it was not relying on echoes to locate its prey.

In another experiment, Payne placed both a dead mouse and a loudspeaker in different places under the leaves. Nothing happened until he turned on the recorded sound. When he did, the owl immediately struck the loudspeaker and ignored the mouse. This experiment strongly suggests that if the owl uses smell to hunt at all, it much prefers to use its hearing.

In a rather conclusive test, Payne used a cotton wad to plug one of the owl's ears. The owl missed the mouse every time. Without full use of both ears, the owl could not find its prey. Payne could now be reasonably sure that the owl was using its ears to locate mice. He repeated this experiment many times with different owls. The results were always the same.

To determine an owl's accuracy in locating mice, Payne tied a dead mouse to the small loudspeaker so that a tape recording of a mouse moving through leaves could be broadcast from under the mouse. He then taped the loudspeaker to a board and covered the board with clay so that the owl would leave its footprints when it struck. If he turned on the recording and dragged the board along the floor, the owl never missed. Apparently, it could adjust to the changing position of the sound as it flew.

To be sure the owl heard no noise during its flight, he attached a wire to the owl's perch. Now the recording would be turned off as soon as the perch moved when the owl took off. The owl would have to depend on its ability to locate the mouse by the sound it heard just before starting its flight. By marking the positions of the owl's perch and the points where it landed, Payne found that for distances up to 7 m (23 ft) the owl never missed the mouse by more than one degree (Figure 6). This means that its biggest error over a 7-m distance was never more than 12 cm (4.8 in). This is just about the size of the owl's outstretched claws.

Interestingly, the owl seems to know its limitations. If the sound made by the "mouse" was more than 7 m away, the owl would land slightly short of the mouse and then wait until it heard another sound before pouncing.

FIGURE 6

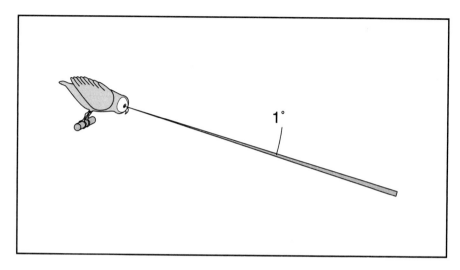

Within 7 m (23 ft) an owl never missed its prey by more than one degree, even in total darkness. At 7 m, an error of one degree is only 12 cm (4.8 in).

To find out how an owl strikes its prey, Payne took movies. First, he filmed an owl with the lights on. His movies showed that after an owl heard the mouse, it turned to face the sound, leaned its head forward, and pushed off from its perch. The owl made one stroke of its wings and then glided straight to the mouse. As it approached its prey, the owl suddenly moved its feet from beneath its tail forward to a point under its chin. Then, at the moment just before striking, it pulled its head back and spread its claws.

Because humans have more difficulty walking a straight line in darkness than in light, Payne thought an owl might strike differently in darkness than in light. To film his owl in darkness, he used a sniperscope. A sniperscope is a device that can form images of objects from the infrared light (heat) they emit. The images appear on a screen similar to a small television screen. A movie camera can be used to take pictures of the screen every 1/24 second. Payne found that in darkness the owl flapped its wings several times, flew more slowly than in light, and swung its feet back and forth as it moved.

Payne reasoned that the owl on its perch hears the sound coming along a different path than the path its feet must follow to reach the mouse. Figure 7a shows how the two paths differ. To place its ears and feet along the same path leading to the prey, the owl leans forward to hear the sound. This places the bird's ears and feet on the same straight-line path to the mouse (Figure 7b). Just before it strikes, the owl swings its feet forward and its head back. This places its feet along the path its ears were following and its ears back where its feet were.

FIGURE 7

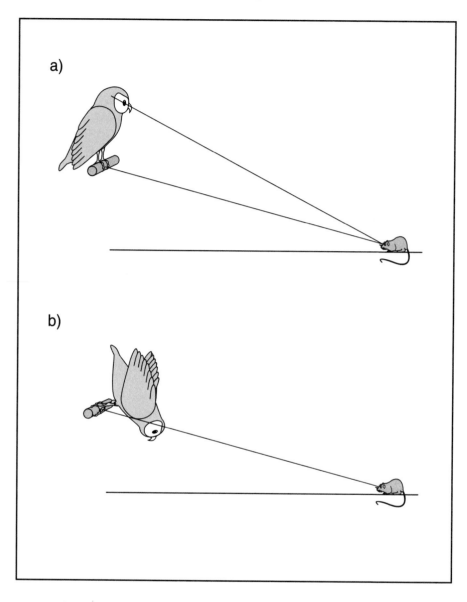

a)

b)

a) The top line shows the straight-line path from the owl's ear to the mouse. The lower line shows the straight-line path from the owl's feet to the mouse.

b) By leaning forward to listen just before it leaves its roost, the owl places its ears and feet on the same path to the mouse.

An owl's claw has four talons that cover a rectangular area (Figure 8). To grasp a mouse most effectively, the owl should be moving across the mouse's path when it strikes (Figure 9) so that its claws reach across the mouse's back. Payne's movies showed that the owl would often turn 90 degrees just before striking the mouse. And it would do this even

FIGURE 8

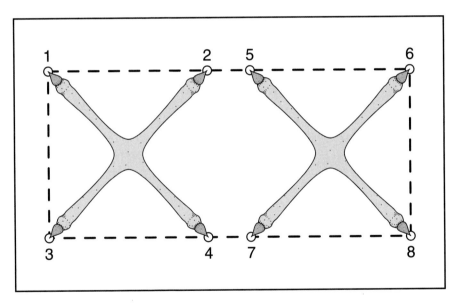

When an owl strikes, the tips of its talons are at the numbered positions shown in the drawing. Roger Payne discovered this pattern by placing a piece of black paper over the loudspeaker he used to send mouse sounds to the owl. When the owl struck, it left holes in the paper. Holes 1, 2, 3, and 4 were made by the owl's left foot. Holes 5, 6, 7, and 8 were made by the bird's right foot.

FIGURE 9

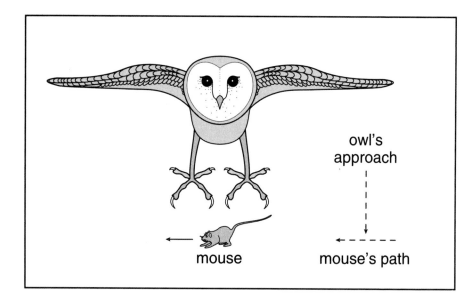

owl's
approach

mouse   mouse's path

An owl is most successful in capturing its prey if it strikes perpendicular to the mouse's path. Its talons will then completely surround the mouse's body.

in darkness. But how can an owl in total darkness know which way a mouse is facing?

Perhaps the owl with its keen sense of hearing can tell the direction the mouse is moving. If it knows the direction the mouse is moving, it knows which way the mouse's body is pointed. To test this idea, Payne used a string to drag a dead mouse along the floor of the totally dark room. He pulled the mouse in different directions. If the mouse was not moving across (perpendicular to) the owl's flight path, the owl would turn just before it struck until it was perpendicular to the path of the mouse.

To be sure the owl was guided by its ears and not its eyes, Payne dragged the mouse sideways, not headfirst, across the floor. The owl still pounced on its prey perpendicular to the direction the mouse was moving even though this was now the worst angle of attack. The owl still "assumed" the mouse's head would be pointed in the direction it was traveling.

Payne wondered if an owl in darkness can judge the distance to its prey with its ears. The fact that it extended its feet just before striking suggested that it can. But because the owl moved more slowly in darkness, flapped its wings, and kept its feet swinging beneath its body, Payne reasoned that it might not know the exact distance to its prey. Perhaps it was judging distance to the floor by the back pressure created by the air it pushed downward with its wing. Perhaps it could tell when it was very close to its prey by smelling it. However, the fact that it would strike a loudspeaker indicated that it did not use its sense of smell. What kind of experiment do you think Payne devised to find out whether an owl can judge distance, not just direction, with its ears?

Experiment *2.1

USING YOUR EARS TO FIND DIRECTION

To do this experiment you will need:

- ✔ tape measure
- ✔ masking tape or marking pen
- ✔ rubber tubing about 1.5 m (5 ft) long (old piece of garden hose works well)
- ✔ a friend
- ✔ small stick
- ✔ two spoons
- ✔ string
- ✔ chair
- ✔ large room
- ✔ blindfold (towel will do)
- ✔ pieces of tape
- ✔ pen

In one of Roger Payne's experiments, he plugged one of the owl's ears with cotton. You may have wondered why plugging only one ear with cotton prevented the owl from locating the mouse. This experiment will help you to understand why an owl needs both ears to find a mouse in darkness.

You can locate objects in space with your own ears. Distant sounds are fainter than sounds that are nearby. Sounds to the left of center reach your left ear slightly before they reach your right ear. Similarly, sounds to the right of center reach your right ear slightly before they reach your left ear. This difference in time for sound to reach your left and right ears allows you to judge the direction from which the sound is coming.

You can easily demonstrate that the difference in time for sound to reach your two ears allows you to determine the sound's direction. Use a tape measure and a piece of masking tape or a marking pen to mark the center of a piece of rubber tubing about 1.5 m (5 ft) long. Place the tubing behind a friend and ask him or her to hold the ends of the tube in his or her ears, as shown in Figure 10. Use a small stick to scratch the tube to the right or left of the center line that you marked. Can your friend tell which ear is closer to the point where the scratch was made? How far to the right of center must the scratch be made before your friend can tell that the sound is coming from the right? How far to the left of center must the scratch be made before your friend can tell that the sound is coming from the left?

To see that someone can determine direction with his or her ears, attach a string to a spoon. Hold the end of the string so that the spoon is suspended. Use a second spoon to strike the suspended spoon. The spoons will serve as your source of sound in this experiment.

FIGURE 10

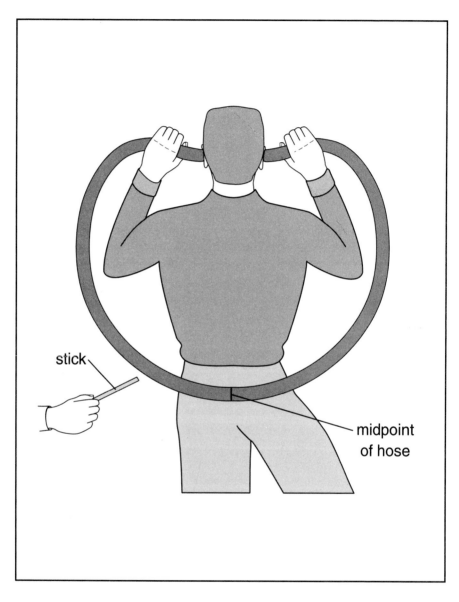

stick

midpoint
of hose

Can you tell whether the scratch is made to the right or left of
center of the hose? The sound travels along the air in the hose.

Place a chair in the center of a large room. Ask a friend to sit on the chair. Explain that you are going to test his or her ability to determine the direction of sound, and that you need to apply a blindfold.

After covering your friend's eyes, be sure that he or she cannot see. Be sure, too, that your friend is facing directly forward. Then use the spoons to generate a sound several meters (yards) directly in front of your friend, as shown in Figure 11. Ask your friend to point to the direction where he or she thinks the sound

FIGURE 11

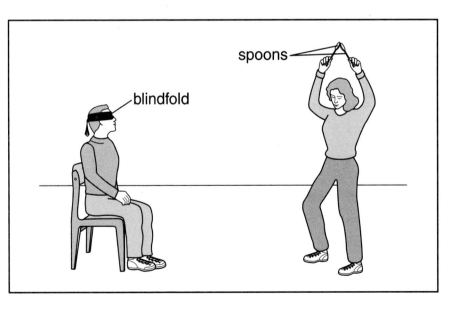

Can a person who is blindfolded tell the direction from which a sound comes?

was made. Next, generate sounds from a number of different positions to the right and left of your friend. How accurately can he or she identify the location of the sounds you make? You might like to mark the position of the sound and the direction your friend points with small pieces of tape on the floor. Label the two corresponding pieces of tape with the same number, and an S (for sound) or P (for pointing). Use different pieces of tape and different numbers for each trial.

Is your friend able to locate sounds best if they come from directly in front? from the left of center? from the right of center? from behind? from the side?

Does the distance to the sound affect your friend's ability to locate its direction? Will a different sound, say one made by snapping your fingers, affect your friend's ability to locate the direction of the sound?

WALKING STRAIGHT, BALANCE, AND DARKNESS

To do this experiment you will need:

- ✔ large empty room
- ✔ a friend
- ✔ small object
- ✔ short length of 2-in x 4-in board

- ✔ watch or clock with second hand
- ✔ paper and pencil
- ✔ pocket calculator (optional)

Roger Payne knew that humans have more difficulty walking a straight line in darkness than in light. He thought an owl might also strike differently in darkness than in light. He said this might be true if both owls and humans find it more difficult to keep their balance in darkness than in light.

Does darkness affect your ability to walk in a straight line? To find out, stand at one end of a large empty room. Have a friend place a small object at the base of the wall on the opposite side of the room. Then walk slowly along a straight-line path to the object, keeping your hands and arms stretched out in front of you. Have your friend stand behind you to judge the straightness of your walk. (The reason for keeping your hands and arms outstretched is to make the conditions the same when you walk in darkness. Then you will want to keep your arms and hands in front of you to avoid bumping into anything.)

Now repeat the experiment with your eyes closed. Your friend will again judge the straightness of your walk and warn you when you are approaching the opposite wall. Repeat this experiment several times. What do you conclude? Do you walk straighter in light than in darkness? What happens when your friend tries this experiment?

To compare your balance in darkness and light, place a short length of a 2-in x 4-in board on the floor. With your eyes open, place one foot on the board and raise your other foot, as shown in Figure 12. Have a friend use a watch or clock with a second hand to measure and record the time that you can remain balanced on one foot. Repeat the experiment while balancing on your other foot. How long can you balance on this foot? Repeat the experiment three times. Determine the average length of time that you can balance on one foot.

Now repeat the experiment with your eyes closed. Determine the average length of time

FIGURE 12

piece of
2 x 4 lumber

How long can you balance your body on a piece of lumber using
only one foot? Can you do as well with your eyes closed?

that you can balance on one foot with your eyes closed. Does darkness affect your ability to keep your balance?

You probably had trouble balancing and walking in a straight line with your eyes closed. Was your difficulty caused by darkness, or was it because your eyes were closed? Design your own experiment to find out.

DID YOU KNOW. . .?

In addition to your eyes, the semicircular canals of your inner ear are essential to maintaining balance. The fluid in these canals pushes on very fine hairs connected to nerve cells. These nerve cells send impulses to your brain and enable you to constantly adjust the muscles that keep your body in balance.

OWL PELLETS

To do this experiment you will need:

- ✔ rubber gloves
- ✔ owl pellets
- ✔ newspaper
- ✔ tweezers
- ✔ magnifying glass
- ✔ a field guide to mammals

As you know, some owls roost in barns. Others roost in trees, church steeples, or cemeteries. If you know a place where owls live, get permission to look around on the ground beneath their roosts. You will probably find matted, hairy, dark wads. These wads, called owl pellets, have an oval shape and are about 5–8 cm (2–3 in) long and half as wide.

Owls have no teeth. They use their hooked beaks to tear their food into pieces that they swallow whole. They cannot digest some parts of the material they eat, such as hair, seed coats, bones, and insect skeletons. They cough up this undigested matter after the rest of their prey has been at least partially digested.

It is the undigested material that makes up the pellets.

Put on some rubber gloves and collect some owl pellets, and take them to your home or school. (If you can't find owl pellets, you can buy some from a science supply house that carries biological materials. Your teacher may have a catalog for such a place.) Place the pellets on an old newspaper. While wearing rubber gloves, use tweezers to pull the pellets apart. Unless very recently regurgitated, the pellets will be dry and odorless. Examine the material inside the pellet with a magnifying glass. Do you find bones? insect skeletons? seed coats? A field guide to mammals will help you identify the animals from which the bones came. What does an owl eat? How are owls adapted to capturing the foods that make up their diet?

Physiological experiment on animals is justifiable for real investigation, but not for mere . . . curiosity.
(Charles Darwin)

3

SOME ANIMALS AND THEIR BEHAVIOR

In this chapter you will examine the behavior of some common small animals as well as two larger animals, including humans. You will start with animals whose behavior is mostly innate. One general rule to follow when working with animals is this: Don't do anything to an animal that you wouldn't do to yourself.

Experiment *3.1

SOW BUGS

To do this experiment you will need:

- ✔ sow bugs
- ✔ paper cup
- ✔ sand
- ✔ peat moss
- ✔ plastic container
- ✔ cardboard
- ✔ deep plastic or cardboard container, about 30 cm (12 in) on a side

- ✔ moist sponge
- ✔ raw potato
- ✔ 3 large jar tops
- ✔ black construction paper
- ✔ lighted place that is not hot

Sow bugs (pill bugs, or wood lice), like the one shown in Figure 13, can be found in damp places. Look under stones, logs, and leaves where they feed on decaying plants. Collect some sow bugs (about 3 dozen) in a paper cup. Keep them in a plastic container in which you have placed a mixture of sand and damp peat moss. Add a moist sponge to the container, and put a cardboard cover over it. About once a week, add a piece of raw potato.

FIGURE 13

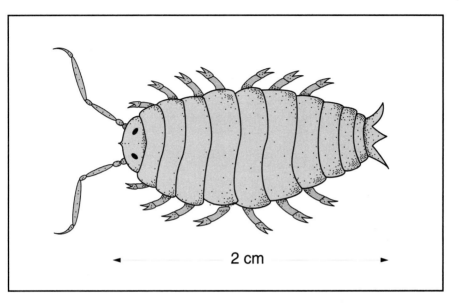

2 cm

Sow bugs, like the enlarged one shown here, are very common.
You might find some in your basement or under a rock.

To find out the kind of environment that
sow bugs prefer, cover the bottom of a plastic
or cardboard container (about 30 cm [12 in] on
a side) with sand. Push three large jar tops
into the sand with their open ends up. The
open tops should be level with the sand, but
empty. Place dry peat moss in one jar top,
moist peat moss in the second, and wet peat
moss in the third. Cover half of each jar top
with black construction paper, as shown in

FIGURE 14

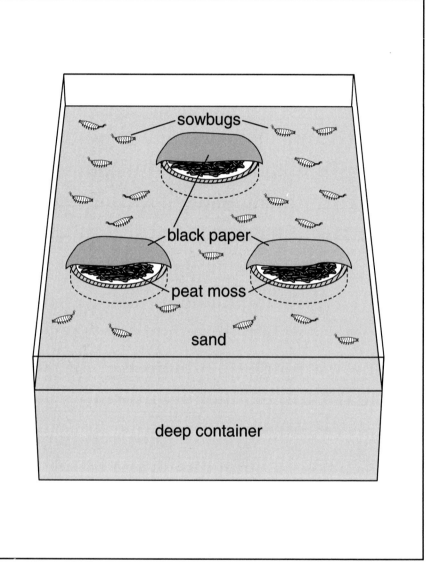

Do sow bugs prefer a dry, damp, or wet environment? Do they prefer light or darkness?

Figure 14. Place about 20 sow bugs on the sand, and put the container in a lighted but not hot place, because sow bugs will die in hot sunlight. (A bright basement, a cool, lighted garage, or a shady place would be good.) During the next day, look for the sow bugs. Are they still wandering around on the sand or have some of them chosen one of the three peat-moss environments? Can you tell which environment they prefer? Do they prefer light or darkness?

Design experiments of your own to find out what kind of temperature (cold, cool, or warm) sow bugs prefer. Can sow bugs smell? Do they respond to touch? Can they hear? Can they learn?

Experiment *3.2

EARTHWORMS IN THE SPOTLIGHT AND IN SOIL

To do this experiment you will need:

- earthworms
- shovel
- Styrofoam cup
- soil
- large shoe box
- cardboard
- scissors
- tape
- clear plastic wrap
- red cellophane or clear red plastic
- paper towels
- window
- cardboard box, about 30 cm (12 in) long, wide, and deep

- dry sand
- damp sand
- dry soil
- damp soil
- dry leaves
- damp leaves
- oatmeal
- spoon
- cotton swab
- vinegar
- ammonia solution (sold in stores as ammonia cleaner)

Find about a dozen earthworms by digging in moist soil. Place the worms in a large Styrofoam cup that holds some soil.

Divide a large shoe box into three parts by taping pieces of cardboard across the box, as shown in Figure 15. The cardboard dividers should not touch the bottom of the box. Leave about a 3-cm (1-in) gap between the cardboard and the bottom of the box so that the worms can crawl under the cardboard. Use scissors to cut square openings in the lid about 8 cm (3 in) on a side above each of the two end compartments.

Tape clear plastic wrap over one opening and several layers of red cellophane or clear red plastic over the other opening. Cover the bottom of the box with moist paper towels.

FIGURE 15

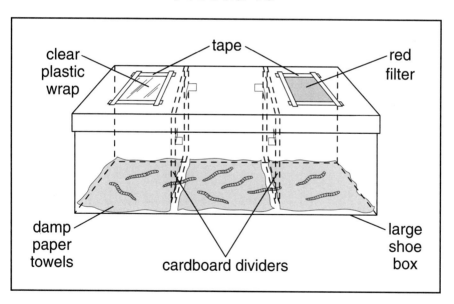

An experiment is shown to find out whether earthworms prefer light or darkness, and how they respond to red light.

Then put a few earthworms in each compartment. Place the box near a window so light can enter the two end compartments. Where are the earthworms after several hours? Are they still evenly distributed among the three compartments or are more in one compartment than another?

Is there any evidence that earthworms respond to light? If there is, do they seem to be attracted to light or repelled by it? Do they respond differently to red light than to ordinary white light? Design an experiment to see if earthworms respond to green or blue light.

Use pieces of cardboard to divide a cardboard box into 6 sections. The dividers should touch the bottom of the box, but they should be only about two-thirds as high as the box (see Figure 16). Into these 6 sections place dry sand, damp sand, dry soil, damp soil, dry leaves, and damp leaves. Be sure the sections are full so that when you put about a dozen earthworms in the box they can crawl along the tops of the different kinds of material and choose the one they want to stay in. Cover the box.

After a day, open the box and use a spoon to carefully remove the sand, soil, and leaves from the different compartments. Record the

FIGURE 16

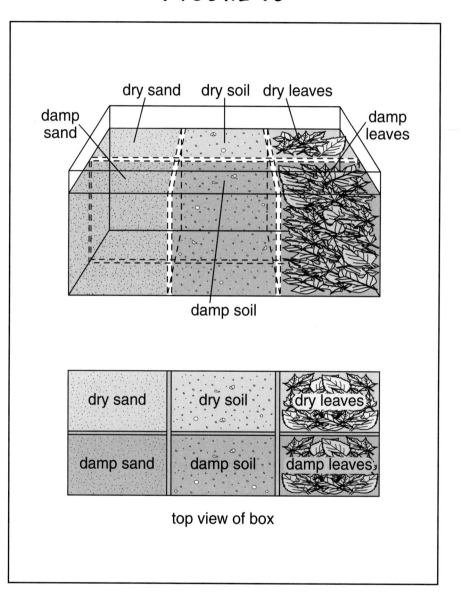

dry sand   dry soil   dry leaves

damp
sand

damp
leaves

damp soil

dry sand	dry soil	dry leaves
damp sand	damp soil	damp leaves

top view of box

Do earthworms prefer dry or damp soil? Which do they like to live in—sand, soil, or dead leaves?

number of earthworms in each type of material. Do earthworms like to live in a dry or a damp environment? Which do they seem to like best—sand, soil, or leaves?

Which environment do you think earthworms would prefer more: the environment you have found they like best, or an environment of oatmeal? Design an experiment to find out.

Design an experiment to discover whether earthworms prefer wet soil or damp soil.

Will earthworms react to vinegar? to ammonia? To find out, place several earthworms on moist paper towels in a box. Dip a cotton swab on a stick into some vinegar. Then hold the wet cotton near (not touching) an earthworm's head and wait. Does the worm react? Do other earthworms react to the vinegar? Do they react to a cotton swab soaked in an ammonia solution? If they react, do you think they react by smelling or touching the chemical?

When you have finished your experiments, return the earthworms to the same place where you dug them up.

Experiment *3.3

MEALWORMS

To do this experiment you will need:

- ✔ mealworms (several dozen)
- ✔ small glass, plastic, or metal container
- ✔ bran or dry cereal such as bran flakes, corn flakes, or wheat flakes
- ✔ paper towel
- ✔ potato or apple
- ✔ shoe box
- ✔ clear plastic tape
- ✔ mirror or clear sheet of rigid plastic
- ✔ clock or watch
- ✔ small glass jar such as baby food jar
- ✔ refrigerator
- ✔ white paper
- ✔ magnifier
- ✔ ruler
- ✔ pencil and paper
- ✔ cardboard
- ✔ paper drinking straw
- ✔ talcum powder
- ✔ flashlight
- ✔ cotton swabs
- ✔ vinegar
- ✔ ammonia solution
- ✔ water
- ✔ pencil or toothpick
- ✔ drinking straw

The Care and Feeding of Mealworms

 You can probably find mealworms under a rotten log in the summer, but it is a lot easier to buy them from a local pet store. They are used as food for a number of animals. Mealworms can also be purchased from a biological supply house. You can keep the worms in a small glass, plastic, or metal container (see Figure 17). Add a handful of bran or a dry cereal such as bran flakes, corn flakes, or wheat flakes to the container. Cover the food with a paper towel. Then put a piece of potato or apple on the towel. The moist food will provide all the water the mealworms need.

Mealworms are the larval stage of the grain beetle. Like many insects, this beetle passes

FIGURE 17

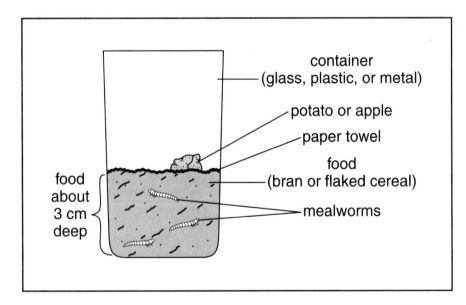

Mealworms are easy to keep. They require little care.

through four distinct stages in its life cycle, as shown in Figure 18. The larval stage lasts about four months. The mealworm then goes into a resting (pupal) stage for about two weeks before the adult beetle emerges. Adult beetles live for several months. Each female will lay about five hundred eggs before she dies. These eggs hatch into mealworms in about a week.

If you would like to watch the life cycle of these beetles, simply change the food supply when the bran or cereal flakes become powdery. Add fresh pieces of potato or apple occasionally to provide moisture. You might like to experiment to find out how temperature, food, moisture, and other factors affect the length of the beetles' life cycle.

Experimenting with Mealworms

Put about 20 mealworms in a shoe box. A strip of clear tape around the top edge of the box will cause them to slip back if they try to crawl out. Just watch the mealworms for a while. You will see that they tend to move along walls and corners.

To see how mealworms move, place one on a mirror or a clear sheet of rigid plastic. How many legs does the mealworm have? How do the legs move as the animal walks? How fast

FIGURE 18

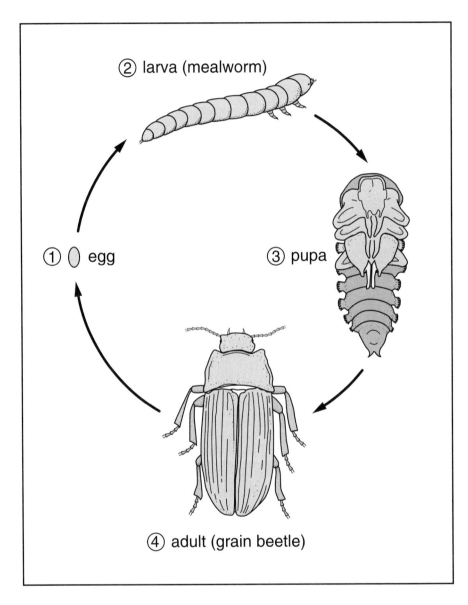

② larva (mealworm)

① egg

③ pupa

④ adult (grain beetle)

Mealworms are the larval stage of the grain beetle, which is an insect. The four distinct stages in its life cycle are: egg, larva (mealworm), pupa, and adult (beetle).

do they walk? How long would it take a mealworm to walk a mile?

Place one or two mealworms in a small glass jar. Put the jar in the refrigerator for a few minutes. The cold air will make the mealworms slow down so that you will be better able to observe them. When the mealworms have become sluggish, remove them from the refrigerator. Put them on a piece of white paper and examine them closely with a magnifier. How long are they? How wide are they? How many segments are in their bodies? Draw a picture of the top and bottom of a mealworm. Can you find their eyes? their antennae? their mouth parts? What do their legs look like? Do they have fine hairs on their body? If so, what might these be used for?

Place a mealworm at the center of a small sheet of cardboard. Raise one side of the cardboard a short distance so the mealworm is on an incline. Which way does the mealworm move? Repeat the experiment at different angles of incline. Does the mealworm always move in the same way? Is the mealworm's motion affected by the angle of the incline?

Place a paper drinking straw on a table. What happens if you place a mealworm headfirst into the drinking straw? What happens if you place him into the straw tailfirst?

How do mealworms find food? Do they see it? smell it? just bump into it by accident? To find out, you might begin by covering the bottom of the shoe box with a very fine layer of talcum powder. Place a small pile of mealworm food (bran or dry cereal flakes) near the center of the box. Then put about a dozen mealworms at one end of the box. As the mealworms move, they will leave tracks in the powder. After the worms have found the food, examine the paths they followed. How do you think they found the food? Do you think they will find the food sooner if you put the food near a wall?

You may have noticed that mealworms sometimes move backwards. What might you do to make a mealworm move backwards? Here are a few things you might try. You may be able to think of some other ways. Try each thing many times and with different mealworms.

- *Shine a flashlight at the mealworm. If the worm backs up, is it because of the light or the flashlight itself?*

- *Dip a small cotton swab on a stick into vinegar. Hold it in front of the mealworm. Repeat the experiment using ammonia solution. Repeat once more with water.*

- *Touch the mealworm gently with a pencil or a toothpick. Does it matter where you touch the worm?*

🐛 *Make a loud noise near the mealworm.*

🐛 *Blow air through a drinking straw at the mealworm. Does it matter where the air hits the mealworm?*

🐛 *Block its path with different kinds of material.*

Which method works best? Is there anything that works every time?

Other Questions to Investigate

Watching mealworms can lead to many more questions about their behavior. A few of these questions are listed below. You may have more of your own.

🐛 *Can mealworms see? If they can, can they see colors?*

🐛 *Will mealworms crawl over the edge of a table and fall, or will they stay along the table's edge?*

🐛 *Can mealworms hear?*

🐛 *Mealworms are often seen crawling along walls. How do they find a wall? How do they sense that the wall is there?*

🐛 *Do mealworms prefer light or darkness?*

🐛 *What food do mealworms like best?*

🐛 *Do mealworms prefer a dry or a moist environment?*

Experiment *3.4

FISH AND TEMPERATURE

To do this experiment you will need:

- ✔ goldfish, preferably Comets
- ✔ aquarium
- ✔ thermometer
- ✔ watch or clock with second hand
- ✔ plastic bag
- ✔ ice cubes

Fish live in water, so they don't breathe air. They obtain their oxygen from the small amount of the gas that is dissolved in water. If you watch a fish (Figure 19a) closely, you will see that it appears to gulp water. But the fish doesn't swallow the water. Instead, the water passes over its gills (Figure 19b). The oxygen in the water enters the blood in the gills. This is similar to the way oxygen passes from air to blood in your lungs.

Unlike you, a fish is cold-blooded. Its body temperature falls when the water it is in cools. To see if temperature affects a fish's gulping (respiration) rate, measure a goldfish's gulping rate in its aquarium. Count the number of

FIGURE 19

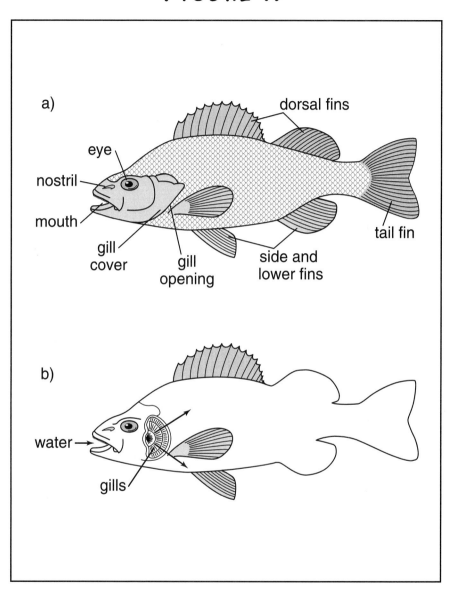

a) The external anatomy of a fish is shown in the drawing.

b) This drawing shows the gills that lie under the gill cover. As water enters the fish's mouth and flows over the many tiny blood vessels in the gills, oxygen passes from the water to the fish's blood. The water then flows outside the fish's body through the gill openings, one on each side of its head.

times it gulps in 30 seconds. Do this several times and take an average.

Use a thermometer to measure the temperature of the water in the aquarium. Then let a plastic bag filled with ice cubes float in the aquarium. When the temperature of the water has fallen 5 degrees Celsius (about 10 degrees Fahrenheit), remove the bag of ice. Again count how many times the same goldfish gulps in 30 seconds. Do this several times and take an average. How does temperature affect a goldfish's gulping rate?

Design your own experiments to answer the following questions: Do goldfish sleep? Can goldfish hear? Do goldfish prefer light or darkness? Can a goldfish be made to swim upside down? Does temperature affect your breathing rate?

Experiment *3.5

BIRD FEEDERS: AN IQ TEST FOR SQUIRRELS

To do this experiment you will need:

✔ birdseed	✔ materials to make a "squirrelproof" bird feeder
✔ squirrels	

If you have a bird feeder, you may know that squirrels enjoy feasting on the seeds you put out for birds. Try to design a bird feeder that you think is "squirrelproof." Then watch the squirrels. Can they find a way to get to the bird feeder?

How do they proceed? Do you think they learn? If they learn, do they learn by trial and error? Or do they learn by insight or thinking? What makes you think so?

Experiment *3.6

EXPERIMENTS WITH THE HUMAN ANIMAL

To do this experiment you will need:

- ✔ people to interview and observe
- ✔ pad of paper and pencil
- ✔ television
- ✔ telephone

Colored Emotions

 Do colors affect our emotions? We certainly respond to colors. A red light tells us to stop. A green light tells us it is safe to go. A yellow light warns us to be cautious. But what emotions, thoughts, or actions do we associate with colors? Do different people respond to colors in the same or different ways?

To find out, interview as many people as possible. Ask, "What do the following colors mean to you?" Then ask them to respond for each color listed in the following chart. Then ask the question, "How do the following colors make you feel (sad, angry, happy, sleepy, etc.)?"

NAME OF PERSON	COLOR						
	WHITE	BLACK	BLUE	GREEN	YELLOW	ORANGE	RED
John Smith							

DO NOT WRITE IN THIS BOOK

Record their answers in a chart like the one above.

Do people respond in similar or different ways to a particular color? Does age affect their responses? Do men and boys respond differently than women and girls?

Body Language

You can often tell how people feel just by watching them. A yawn may indicate that someone is bored or tired. A smile may indicate happiness or it may be a conditioned response to meeting someone new. Other actions might include shrugging, looking away, laughing, frowning, shouting, sticking out a tongue, etc.

Study people as you sit down at your family dinner table. Can you tell by looking whether someone is happy, sad, angry, bored, or annoyed? Do their words later confirm what you thought by just looking?

People usually use body language when they are responding to another person, an object, or a situation. Try watching people in a library, store, airplane terminal, classroom, dinner table, or any place where you can observe them. Sit far enough away so that you cannot hear what is said. Don't stare—unless you want to see how someone responds when you do!

As you "people watch," make a table of your observations. Record the action you see, the message you think it sends, the response (if any) of someone receiving the message, and the message (if any) sent by the receiver. One example is given in the short table below.

ACTION	MESSAGE	RESPONSE	RETURN MESSAGE
Smile	Hi, friend!	Smile	Good to see you too!

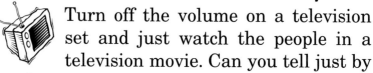

Silent Television and Invisible People

Turn off the volume on a television set and just watch the people in a television movie. Can you tell just by watching how they feel about one another? If you can, what clues are you using?

Can you tell what the movie is about just by watching? If you can, what signs are helping you to understand the story?

When you talk on the telephone, you can't see the person with whom you are talking. What can you learn from the person's voice? Can you tell if he or she is happy? sad? angry? in a hurry? eager to talk?

DID YOU KNOW. . .?

A person's pupil (the black part of the eye at the center of the colored iris) dilates when viewing something pleasant or interesting. The dilation is a reflex action well known to accomplished poker and bridge players.

Experiment *3.7

USING YOUR NOSE

To do this experiment you will need:

✔ a friend	✔ perfume
✔ blindfold	✔ table

Many animals, such as dogs, rely on their sense of smell more than their vision or hearing. To see how well you can use your own sense of smell, ask a friend to blindfold you. Then, while you wait, have your friend open a bottle of perfume and place it in an open place on a table near one side of a nearby room.

Your friend will then lead you into the room. Once there, you will try to locate the perfume by "following your nose." Your friend will warn you if you are about to bump into something. But you are to use your nose to find the perfume if you can. Can your nose lead you to the perfume? How well can your friend do? Would you be better able to find a ticking clock? How else might you test your sense of smell?

Helen Keller, who was both deaf and blind, could readily identify people by their odor. To people who rely on their noses, instead of their eyes and ears as most of us do, a person's odor is as distinct as his or her appearance or voice.

Can you identify people by their odor? Design an experiment to find out.

Design an experiment to find out if your sense of smell is better when you are blindfolded or in darkness. Design another experiment to find out if your sense of hearing is better when you are blindfolded or in darkness.

Experiment *3.8

... Z Z Z ...

SLEEPY TIMES

To do this experiment you will need:

- ✔ dogs, cats, and other animals
- ✔ a friend
- ✔ clock or watch

How much time do you spend sleeping each day? Do animals sleep as much as you do? To find out, you and a friend can divide the time needed to watch a dog or cat throughout the day. How much time does a dog sleep each day? How much time does a cat sleep each day?

If possible, watch other animals. What fraction of each day do they spend sleeping? Is the amount of time an animal sleeps related to its age? Do male animals sleep more or less than female animals? Do most animals sleep more or less than humans?

Learned of every bird its language,
Learned their names and all their secrets,
Talked with them whene'er he met them.
(Henry Wadsworth Longfellow)

4
DO ANIMALS TALK?

We communicate mostly by talking, but there are other ways to communicate. A person who is deaf cannot hear spoken words coming from a television set. But he or she may be able to understand what is said by reading the speaker's lips or watching someone who is signing (using hands and arms to send signals that represent words).

We are unable to carry on a two-way conversation with animals that are not human. And there is no conclusive evidence that animals can talk to one another by using speech. However, animals do appear to be able to communicate in a variety of ways. In fact, parrots, as you will learn, may be able to talk with humans though not to one another.

Alarm Calls

 People who have watched vervet monkeys in East Africa believe that these primates have four different calls to alert one another. Recordings show that each kind of call warns the other monkeys about a different kind of predator. Upon hearing one type of call, the monkeys will look up as they take cover under bushes. This call is believed to indicate the presence of hawks or eagles who will attack them. A second call leads the animals to immediately find and climb a tree. This call probably indicates a walking predator such as a leopard. After hearing a third type of call, the monkeys look toward the ground. This call is believed to indicate that a snake is nearby. A fourth alarm call causes these primates to hide and may indicate the approach of a group of predators such as humans.

Field experiments show that the monkeys do respond to the alarm call and not just to the predator. If a recording of the alarm call is broadcast when no predators are about, the animals respond as they would to a call by another monkey.

The calls appear to be innate; however, some learning is involved. Young vervets will make the calls when they see harmless birds, falling leaves, and any mammal. As a result, adult vervets seldom react to alarm calls made by the young. As the young vervets grow older, they become more selective and appear to learn which birds and mammals are dangerous.

A Talking Bird

You might think that chimpanzees, the primates most closely related to humans, might be able to talk. But these animals cannot form words. Parrots can, however, and "Polly want a cracker" is not all they can say. Parrots can talk, but do they understand what they are saying?

For instance, if a parrot learns to say "sunflower seeds," it will ask for sunflower seeds when hungry. It may also reject a different food that is offered. Although the parrot seems to understand the words, this may only be an example of conditioned learning. The parrot has learned that saying

FIGURE 20

A parrot can say words that you would recognize. But does it know what it is saying?

the words "sunflower seeds" is followed by food. It may reject a substitute only because it does not like that food as well.

Among humans, children learn sounds by listening to adults. So in one long-term experiment two people talked slowly to one another every day in the presence of a parrot. One person would hold an object and ask, "What's this?" The second person would get the object when he or she responded with the correct name, color, shape, or whatever was being taught. After ten years, the parrot knew seventy words. It could name thirty objects, seven colors, five shapes, and five numbers, and could even speak a few phrases. It could also tell its trainer the color of an object it had never seen before. This shows that the parrot understood the concept of color as distinct from objects.

Although chimpanzees can't form words that we recognize, they may communicate by sound. Chimps tend to cluster in small groups as they move through the jungle. Field studies suggest that these groups communicate with one another over large distances by making distinctive calls. The two-way nature of the exchange may indicate some kind of conversation similar to human language.

Gestures, Sign Language, Symbols, and Animals

 Sea lions have been trained to respond to almost two hundred human gestures. Unlike parrots, sea lions cannot speak, and their anatomy restricts their gesture vocabulary.

Dolphins have been trained to respond to both words and gestures. Although their vocabulary is less than forty "words," they seem to be able to understand simple sentences. In response to the sentence "Bottom pipe put in hoop," a dolphin will pick up a small pipe on the bottom of its pool and put it in a hoop near the side of the pool. They can distinguish between "Hoop, fetch, ball" and "Ball, fetch, hoop." (The first sentence means "find the hoop and carry it to the ball"; the second means "find the ball and carry it to the hoop.")

Some scientists think that dolphins and whales can communicate with one another. They believe the clicks, whistles, squeals, and squawks that these animals make have meaning to members of the same species who hear them. It is likely that these sounds have meaning, but there is no conclusive evidence that these water-dwelling mammals can talk to one another the way we do.

There is good evidence that, like bats, toothed whales (including dolphins) use high-pitched sounds to scan their surroundings. By turning their heads as they produce these sounds, dolphins sweep the area around them. This is much like the radar sweeps made by traffic control towers at airports. The dolphins may use the returning echoes to create sound images of objects, just as we use reflected light to create visual images of objects. Their sound images are probably not as sharp as our visual images, but they are more penetrating. They might resemble the images formed when doctors use ultrasound to examine hearts or babies who are still inside their mothers.

One of the most fascinating sounds is the song of male humpback whales. The whales release no air as they sing; no bubbles can be seen rising through the water. The sound probably comes from air vibrating in their lungs, mouths, and sinuses. The songs are made up of themes sung in a fixed order. Played at a faster speed, they sound like a bird's song. While the song is the same for all members of a herd, it is slightly different for different herds. Furthermore, the song changes slowly from one year to the next.

Because the song can last for thirty minutes, the whales must be able to remember the "words." Katherine Payne and Linda Guinee studied the sound patterns in these songs. They found patterns that seemed to be repeated, much as we might form rhymes. Rhyming helps us to remember songs and poems. Payne and Guinee think humpbacks may use rhyming too. The fact that rhyming patterns are more frequent in longer humpback songs supports their belief.

Why do humpbacks sing at all? No one knows. But the fact that the songs are sung by males during the mating season suggests they are love songs.

B. T. and R. A. Gardner spent four years with a chimpanzee named Washoe. They were able to teach Washoe 130 words using American Sign Language, the language used by the deaf. Washoe and other chimps could identify objects on a screen and use sign language to show that they knew the objects.

The chimps were also able to use the words they had learned in different settings. For example, Washoe used gestures to call a swan "water bird." A cigarette lighter was called "metal hot," a seltzer tablet dropped into water was referred to as "listen drink," and a watermelon was called "candy drink." Washoe learned the sign for "open" to mean "open a door," but she used the word as well when referring to a book, a faucet, and drawers. These examples show that chimps can use a language they have learned in ways that seem to require some thought.

There is also evidence that chimps can use sign language to communicate with one another. Washoe taught her adopted son, Loulis, fifty signs over a four-year period.

David Premack used colored plastic shapes like the ones drawn in Figure 21 as symbols for words. He was able to teach a chimp named Sarah to understand sentences such

FIGURE 21

Some chimpanzees can learn the meaning of symbols like the ones shown here.

as those shown in the drawing. Sarah learned over 100 symbols and could use them in three- or four-word sentences. Once a chimp learns to associate a plastic symbol (word) with an object or action, it takes less time to teach new associations. The same is true for humans. A chimp can also learn to use a symbol to mean a whole class of objects, not just a single object. This is much like a baby who learns that the word "man" has a broader meaning than "dada." However, not all chimps can be taught to use symbols. And those that can, learn only about two words a month. In contrast, young children may learn more than a dozen new words each day.

It has also been possible to teach chimpanzees to communicate by using a keyboard with keys made up of the symbols they recognize as words. Some of these chimps are able to use keyboards to communicate with one another. One young chimp watched his mother use a keyboard through two years of training. Without any formal training of his own, he was able to use the keyboard. In fact, he seemed to use it more effectively than his mother did. Similarly, you may find it easier to use a computer than a parent or grandparent does. It seems clear that some chimps understand that symbols can be used to exchange information and communicate wishes. They can use these symbols in much the same way that we use written words.

Bee Language

One of the last places you might expect to find language is among insects. Their brains are tiny, and we certainly don't think of them as intelligent. Yet, more than fifty years ago Karl von Frisch discovered the dancing language of bees.

Early in the twentieth century, von Frisch had shown that bees are not color-blind. Although they cannot see red, they can be trained to find food on the basis of color. Other experiments led him to believe that bees communicate. When he placed a sugar solution some distance from a hive, a bee would eventually discover the sugar and return to the hive. Shortly after its return, a large number of bees would fly from the hive to the sugar.

To try to understand how bees communicate, von Frisch built special hives with glass covers. The clear glass allowed him to watch the bees closely. By tagging bees with dots of paint, he learned that bees returning to the hive from a rich source of food moved in unusual ways, which he called dancing.

The bees performed two kinds of dance. In one dance the bees moved in tight circles; in another, they waggled their abdomens as they ran a short distance, then turned and returned to their starting position. Figure 22 shows a bee's path for these two dances. Other bees in the hive are excited by the nectar on the dancing bees and fly out in search of the same food source. The odor of the nectar, pollen, or experimental sugar solution helps them to find the particular food source discovered by the dancer.

To learn the meaning of the dances, von Frisch trained two groups of bees from the same hive to feed at separate places. The first group, identified by a blue paint, fed at a station only a couple of meters (yards) from the hive. The second group, stained with a red paint, fed at a place 300 meters from the hive. He found that all the blue bees did the circle dance; the red bees did the waggle dance.

Next, he slowly moved the food source for the red bees closer to the hive. At the same time he slowly moved the food source for the blue bees farther away. When their food source reached a point 50 to 100 meters from the hive, the red bees began to use a circle dance rather than the waggle dance. When the blue bees' food source was moved between 50 and

FIGURE 22

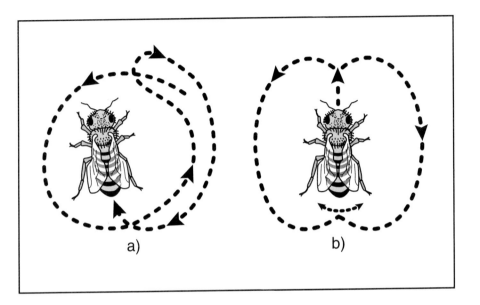

Bees communicate by "dancing."

a) The dashed lines and arrows show the path followed by a bee doing the circle dance.

b) The lines and arrows show the path followed by a bee doing the waggle dance.

100 meters from the hive, their dance changed from a circle to a waggle dance. It was clear to von Frisch that the circle dance indicated a nearby food source. The waggle dance indicated that the food was more than 50 to 100 meters from the hive. Furthermore, if the food was 100 meters away, the dancing bee would make about ten short waggle runs in

fifteen seconds. If the food was farther away, it would make fewer but longer waggle runs in the same time. For food 3,000 meters away it would make only three long waggle runs in fifteen seconds.

Von Frisch found that the bees seldom flew in the wrong direction. Somehow they had been "told" the direction of the food source. But how did the bees know in which direction to fly after observing the waggle dance?

Von Frisch captured a few bees on their return flights to the hive. If released soon after they were caught, the bees would fly straight to the hive. But if they were kept in the dark for several hours, they would fly in the wrong direction when released. He noticed that the direction of their flight was at the same angle to the sun that it had been when they were placed in the dark. The sun had moved about thirty degrees between their capture and release. The bees were now off target by about thirty degrees in seeking their hive.

These experiments led von Frisch to believe that dancing bees were able to "tell" other bees the direction of the food source as measured from the sun. The directional information is most clearly seen on hot days when the dance is done on a flat landing in front of the hive. Here the straight part of the waggle dance points directly at the target food (see Figure 23a). On cooler days, the dance is performed on a vertical honeycomb inside the hive. The dancer uses a maplike approach to tell the other bees about direction, using the sun as a reference point. On this "map," the direction of the sun is always understood to be vertical—toward the top of the honeycomb. If the food is in the same direction as the sun, the straight part of the bee's waggle dance will be straight up the comb (see Figure 23b). If the food is along a line 60 degrees to the left of the sun, the straight part of the bee's waggle dance will be 60 degrees to the left of the vertical (see Figure 23c).

In his first experiments, von Frisch used the Austrian honeybee. In later experiments with other species of honeybees, von Frisch found that different species "speak" different "dialects." The change from circle dance to waggle dance occurs at different distances for different species. The number of straight waggle runs per fifteen seconds and the length of the run indicate different distances for different species. For food at a distance of 500 meters, the Austrian honeybee will make about six waggle runs in fifteen seconds. The Indian honeybee will make about half as many. The dwarf honeybee can dance only on a

FIGURE 23

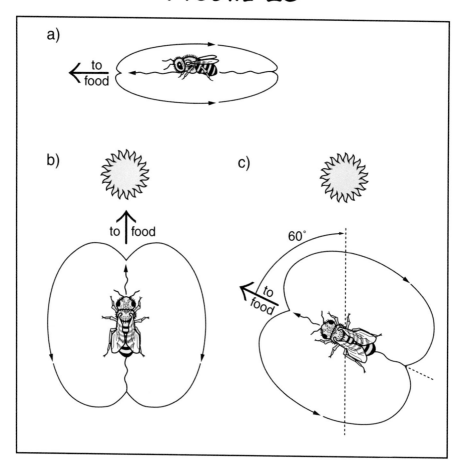

Honeybees use the waggle dance to communicate the direction of a food source.

a) On a horizontal surface, the bee's waggling motion is aimed directly toward the food source.

b) On a vertical honeycomb, the direction of the sun is always understood to be straight up the comb, just as north is always at the top of the maps we use. If the food is in the same direction as the sun, the bee will move straight up the honeycomb as it waggles.

c) If the food is 60 degrees to the left of the sun, the bee will move along a line 60 degrees to the left of the vertical as it waggles.

horizontal (flat) surface. It will not dance on a vertical surface. One species, a tiny stingless bee, does not dance at all. A forager who has found food simply moves around the hive excitedly, bumping into other bees who then fly out seeking the odor they smelled on the forager who bumped into them. Because they have no clue as to the direction of the food, it takes them much longer to find the food. But it was bees like these who probably preceded the dancing bees in the long evolution of bee language.

The bees' dancing language is clear and filled with useful information, but it is an innate behavior, not a learned one. To be certain of this, von Frisch took honeycombs from a hive and raised the young bees away from the adults. When the young bees were brought back to the hive, they were able to react to the dance of other bees immediately. They could fly in the correct direction to find food. They could perform dances on their own identical to those of the older bees who had lived in the hive all their lives. The dancing language of bees is in their genes; they do not learn it.

Experiment *4.1

HONEYBEE TALK

To do this experiment you will need:

- ✔ area with bees and flowers
- ✔ honey
- ✔ plate
- ✔ binoculars
- ✔ watch

IF YOU ARE ALLERGIC TO BEE STINGS, DO NOT DO THIS EXPERIMENT! As you know, honeybees are able to tell other bees where to find a good source of pollen or nectar. It's not easy to watch bees do their dance, but you can see the effects of their communication.

In the fall, when bees are searching for nectar before temperatures drop, look for an area where bees have found some flowers. Pour some honey on a plate and put it near the flowers. Stand far enough away so there are no bees near you. Use binoculars to watch the plate of honey.

Notice the time on your watch when one or more bees discover the honey. How long is it before a lot of bees arrive at the honey? Using your binoculars, you may be able to watch the bees fly to and from their hive. **DO NOT GO NEAR THE HIVE!**

DID YOU KNOW. . .?

Male honeybees are called drones. They develop from unfertilized eggs laid by the queen. Their sole purpose is to fertilize the queen's eggs. Before winter sets in, the drones are ejected from the hive and left to starve.

Both queen and worker bees develop from fertilized eggs, but the bee larva destined to be the queen is fed a special diet.

INVENTING YOUR OWN SET OF LANGUAGE SIGNALS

To do this experiment you will need:

✔ pencil and paper   ✔ a friend

If you have played charades, you know how difficult it is to communicate an idea without talking or writing. Native American tribes developed a sign language to help them communicate. The deaf use the American Sign Language (ASL). You may have seen ASL being used on television.

Together with a friend, see if you can develop your own sign language. For example, pointing to yourself could mean "I" or "me," tugging your ear could mean "hear" or "listen," and a clenched fist could mean "I'm angry!" Record your signs on paper as your language grows and changes. Do you ever reach a point where your sign language is complete?

Once you have developed your own sign language, compare it with ASL or the sign language developed by Native American tribes.

FURTHER READING

Aymar, Brandt. *The Personality of the Cat*. Avenel, N.J.: Random House Value, 1989.

Bailey, Jill, and Tony Seddon. *Animal Vision*. New York: Facts on File, Inc., 1988.

Darling, David. *Could You Ever Speak Chimpanzee?* Old Tappan, N.J.: Macmillan Child Group, 1991.

Facklam, Margery. *Do Not Disturb: The Mysteries of Animal Hibernation and Sleep*. Boston: Little, Brown, and Co., 1989.

Flegg, Jim. *Animal Builders*. Brookfield, Conn.: Newington Press, 1991.

———. *Animal Communication*. Brookfield, Conn.: Newington Press, 1991.

Gardner, Robert. *Experimenting with Sound*. New York: Franklin Watts, 1991.

———. *The Whale Watchers' Guide*. New York: Julian Messner, 1984.

Goodman, Billy. *Animal Homes and Societies*. Boston: Little, Brown, and Co., 1992.

Lorenz, Konrad Z. *King Solomon's Ring*. Alexandria, Va.: Time-Life, 1980.

McGrath, Susan. *The Amazing Things Animals Do*. Washington, D.C.: National Geographic Society, 1989.

Parker, Steve. *Camouflage*. New York: Gloucester Press, 1991.

Parker, Steve, and Jane Parker. *Territories*. New York: Gloucester Press, 1992.

Payne, Roger. *How Barn Owls Hunt*. St. Louis: McGraw-Hill, Webster Division, 1968.

Taylor, Barbara. *The Animal Atlas*. New York: Knopf Books for Young Readers, 1992.

Webster, David. *Track Watching*. New York: Franklin Watts, 1972.

———. *Spider Watching*. New York: Julian Messner, 1984.

LIST OF MATERIALS

A
ammonia solution
apple
aquarium

B
baby food jar
bell
binoculars
birdseed
blindfold
board
bran or dry cereal

C
calculator
cardboard
cats
chair
clock
cotton swab

D
dog
drinking straw

E
earthworms

F
field guide for mammals
flashlight
friend

G
goldfish

H
honey

I
ice cubes

J
jar tops

L
leaves

M
magnifying glass
masking tape
mealworms
mirror

N
newspaper

O
oatmeal

owl pellets

P
pad
paper
paper cup
paper towels
peat moss
pen
pencil
people
perfume
plastic bag
plastic container
plastic sheet
plastic wrap
plate
potato

R
red cellophane or plastic
refrigerator
rubber gloves
rubber tubing
ruler

S
sand
scissors
shoe box

shovel
soil
sow bugs
sponge
spoon
squirrels
stick
string
Styrofoam cup

T
table
talcum powder
tape
tape measure
telephone
television
thermometer
toothpick
tweezers

V
vinegar

W
watch
whistle
window

INDEX

WHAT IT MEANS TO BE
SERIES

PUBLISHER	Joseph R. DeVarennes
PUBLICATION DIRECTOR	Kenneth H. Pearson
ADVISORS	Roger Aubin
	Robert Furlonger
EDITORIAL MANAGER	Jocelyn Smyth
EDITORS	Ann Martin
	Shelley McGuinness
	Robin Rivers
	Mayta Tannenbaum
ARTISTS	Summer Morse
	Barbara Pileggi
	Steve Pileggi
	Mike Stearns
PRODUCTION MANAGER	Ernest Homewood
PRODUCTION ASSISTANTS	Catherine Gordon
	Kathy Kishimoto
PUBLICATION ADMINISTRATOR	Anna Good

Canadian Cataloguing in Publication Data

Prasad, Nancy
  What it means to be—proud

(What it means to be; 16)
ISBN 0-7172-2244-6

1. Self-respect — Juvenile literature.
I. Pileggi, Steve.   II. Title.   III. Title: Proud.   IV. Series.

BJ1533.S3P73 1987   j179'.9   C87-095058-4